How to Make Anyone Fall in

Stay in Lo

200 Love Techniques

Demystifying the Laws of Enchantment

How to Make Anyone Fall Madly in Love with You and Stay in Love Copyright ©2016 by Venus Potter

Other Books from this Publishing House:

How to Get Rid of Any Disease, Including Cancer Permanently

More than 50 Scientifically Proven Therapies that cost almost nothing and Will Make You Healthy with No Side Effects

Victoria Parker

Over 60 Breakthrough Anti-Aging Treatments Which Can Make You Decades Younger

Plus: 28 Anti Aging Foods & Elixirs
Plus: 15 Breakthrough Discoveries Will Keep You Forever Young

Victoria Parker

How To Get Anything You Want

The Ultimate Secrets on How To Get Money, Love, Luck and Health

Getting the Mystery of Success Solved

Victoria Parker

You just lost the man you love recently and can't get over him? Or maybe looking for new love?

The best thing that could happen to any of us is to meet the right partner and spend the rest of our lives in a pure bliss. It is also the most difficult thing to happen. That's why the most important goal in anyone's life should be to meet that special person. Most people understand that only after they have already achieved all other goals in their lives.

Meeting The One could happen in a magic way, just like it does in the movies, but most probably, you will have to take the matter in your own hands and help your fate a bit.

A legend says: Once upon a time, there were no men and women – people had bodies, combining male and female sexes. Since they didn't need anyone in order to feel complete, they were very strong. The Gods were scared that someday people would become just like them. So Zeus sent a wind to Earth, which was so strong, that it split each person into two parts – male and female and each part got blown away at a different place around the world. Since that day, each female part is looking for its' own male half. And since both parts have spent so much time away from each other, even though they've met their own half, they still have to work on the relationship even when they are both true soul mates.

Some people meet that other half earlier in life, some later and some never do. Others believe they've met that special person, but in a few months or years, they find out they've just projected their own dreams and illusions onto another person, who has failed to get anywhere close to those expectations.

We all want a perfect ending to the present stories of our lives. It's great to meet your soul mate, but when you get obsessed with searching for perfection, you are guaranteed to fail. While it's Okay to reach up for the stars, it's important we learn to be happy with the perfect imperfections of the ones we love.

Is there really a formula for finding and attracting The One and Only? If you are trying to find some piece of logic in a man's behavior and rely on his rational thinking, you will end up disappointed. Attracting and swiping a man off his feet requires certain skills, which can be learnt. Skills, which can help you meet and keep Mr. Right. Eventually, he will love everything about you, even all those qualities, from which every other man has been scared of so far. And achieving that is easier than you think.

Women are divine species and while part of them will be always searching for Prince Charming, they can also create one.

If you've lived in New York, you would have certainly noticed that many men have an over-inflated sense of self importance. They feel that if they commit to a woman, they actually reject all other alternatives they have and might be missing out on something better. Any man is way more likely to commit even while not yet ready, once he believes he has met his soul mate or trophy wife. But many men out there pass on amazing and extraordinary women while believing they are not yet ready, just to end up marrying an average Plain Jane a few years later, who skillfully tricks them into it.

The more you have to offer, the harder it is to meet the right person.

According to the Law of Attraction, if you are a good person, you will attract another good person and the better person you become, the better partner you will attract. It would be easy if things worked that way – we would have all known what to do if we wanted to attract a good partner. Unfortunately, that is not the case when it comes to love affairs and there are millions of examples to prove it – good people being in a relationship with users, manipulators, con artists, etc. So many good people are being used by cheaters, scammers and liars.

Nowadays, everyone has too many options and dating is even more difficult than ever. Unless a man is seriously interested in you, and you are his top priority, you would both hardly ever get together, as he would be busy choosing between all the women on all the dating apps and dating sites out there, all the invites for events on social media and the last minute texts from friends about parties going on.

Any human being has experienced rejection and we have all felt hurt. It's not a pleasant feeling. It's actually very painful and many people feel physical pain when rejected. Emotional pain may last for many years. Some people even stop functioning because of fear of rejection. No one wants to feel not wanted and not valued. Rejection affects our self-esteem. If you are positive and don't expect rejection, you are less likely to get it. The lower your self-esteem is, the worse you will be able to deal with rejection. The more problems in your life you have – the more vulnerable you will be and the more rejection will hurt. People with high self-esteem are more resilient to rejection. Many people avoid asking someone out just because they are too scared of rejection and they don't want to deal with it.

If your life isn't looking like much of a fairy tale, this book will help you do whatever is needed to get whatever you want, whether you have stumbled upon the man of your dreams already, or you are still searching.

Men are way less complicated and far less smart than women when it comes to romantic matters. There is no relation between how smart a guy is in making money and his expertise in love affairs. Usually, the smartest men, who make most money, are the silliest ones when it comes to love and they are the ones, who fall for the wrong woman in most of the cases. And by the wrong woman, I mean the one, who would be with them for their money only and who would leave them the moment the money is gone and they have to face battering the storm together. Divorce rate is higher than 50% in cities like New York and there are many couples, who stay married just because of children or because of convenience, but they actually feel miserable together. Usually, men who went to Ivy League Schools and make millions a year are the most naïve ones, when it comes to picking the right partner in life. So many strong women and men, who are at the top of their game professionally, feel otherwise powerless when it comes to love.

Women often assume that all men are the same and like the same things. Truth is that women actually pick the same type of men each time based on their past experiences. Quite often, those choices are very toxic, and even though women know it, they are still attracted to that same kind of men over and over again. Same pattern repeats each time. According to psychiatrists, our relationships later in life mirror the ones with our parents. If your parents made you feel insignificant, you will always crave attention, and at the same time always pick the partners, who are not able to give it to you. And if you associate love with pain from your childhood, you would only be able to choose partners, causing pain in all its forms. Or you will be choosing partners, who require rescuing and fixing.

Many people think they know what they want when it comes to relationships, but truth is that they know perfectly well what they don't want, but they don't know what they want. And most often we sabotage our relationships ourselves. We usually do it unconsciously, of course.

Once you read this book, you will know how to stop sabotaging and create an incredible bond instead. You will know how to make anyone fall in love with you.

CHAPTER I

BEFORE YOU MEET HIM:

Before we go the Love Techniques described in this book, here are 22 common sense things and you certainly know them, but I want to remind them to you.

1. Learn that men are different and there is no such thing as one technique that works on all men. Some men are mature and some are not. There are techniques, which would work on an insecure man, who is trying to validate his ego all the time, but a quality man would easily get turned off by the same

thing and you would never see him again. This is described in more details further in the book.

2. Shift your mindset to abundance and be positive about dating. There are many great men out there! When your brain is set up to abundance mode, everything is possible at any time. Believe that he will show up in your life and then he will. Because that's what you really deserve.

3. Don't pay too much attention to what men say, but rather watch their actions. Men often say things they don't mean and they have their own reasons to do so. It is only actions that matter. And there are always many reasons for the decisions men make. It's never just one. When you meet a man, let his actions speak to you instead of his words. Too many men talk big. Talk is cheap.

4. When someone likes you, you will know it. If you are wondering whether he likes you or not, he probably doesn't. A man who likes you will ask you out and will not give up on you easily. If a man is inconsistent, forget about him. Such men are a waste of time.

5. Don't delay living your life for another day, when you will look better or will be smarter. Show up and meet the world out there today and live fully. Don't hold up for next week or next month.

6. People tend to believe that beauty is a physical quality, while it is completely energetic indeed. So feel beautiful and you will look more beautiful. But still, make sure you've done the best you can when it comes to looks. Men like different shapes and sizes and there are no rules on this, but most of them are attracted to women, who have long hair and wear high heels. You could certainly meet him when you have put zero efforts in your looks – running in the park early in the morning, but try to look the best you can as often as possible.

7. According to scientists we are attracted to people, who we think would respond to our feelings most. We are also attracted to those, who look like us, as well as to people, who look like our parents. So if you look like his mother for example, it's a guarantee he will love you. I know a couple, who had sex the first time they met and against all odds, married soon after. Turned out she looked exactly like his mother.

8. Despite all the advices you hear and what you might have read before, you should allow yourself to start talking to a man first, in which case you become the chooser, not the one, who gets chosen. It shows you are confident. You should capture the people you want in your life instead of

sitting and waiting for them to approach you. And yes, I know many couples, who married shortly after they met. And guess what – the woman was the one to approach the man first.

9. If he has been texting you for more than 2 weeks without making any plans to meet, just move on. He is probably talking to tens or even hundreds of women or he is in a relationship.

10. Our perception of reality is subjective and it is not equal to what reality objectively as a matter of fact is. We interpret everything through our points of view and we quite often misunderstand, misinterpret and miscommunicate, which is the reason most relationships fail.

11. Not many men out there are keepers. Try to learn how to recognize the good ones right away. Lean to like men, who are reliable, caring and kind. There are so many men, who are deeply damaged and unfortunately, they are the ones, who are always single and available. You should date someone, whom you respect and admire, not someone who needs to be fixed. You should be with the person, who makes you happy and inspires you, instead of the one, who makes you unhappy. You should break the cycle of picking the wrong guy and

if you have been choosing that particular type in the past, you should not allow your past define you.

12.   Work on becoming a better person every day. Not that most men would appreciate it, but do it for yourself and for the ones, who would eventually recognize it. An amazing man would only be looking to meet an amazing woman. A great book I recommend is "How to Make Every Day Exceptionally Lucky" by Victoria Fairchild Porter (Amazon.com).

13.   Try to show up at the place, where your soul mate could be at this moment. Be at the club, at the store, at the café, in the gym, go on a trip. Use social media.

14.   Remember that you are worthy of love and respect. Stay away from men, who disrespect you.

15.   Once you are happy, joyful and have your life put together, you will attract the right person. He will find you no matter where you are.

16.   Be open to your partner showing into your life in a different way and in a different look from what you would normally expect. We usually restrict our options to "our type" and we never get the chance to explore someone, with whom it might have worked the best and forever.

17. In order to meet the love of your life, you have to be ready. Only when you are ready will you meet him. It's a matter of a mindset. Once both you and the other person are ready, you will not only meet each other, but will also stay together. Get rid of all the thoughts that stop you from being in a relationship. Get rid of all your negative emotions and limiting beliefs, as otherwise you sabotage the relationship subconsciously yourself. Heal yourself from all the damaging thoughts you are stuck with and move forward.

18. Men like to always pass any kind of blame to someone else - no bad thing is ever their fault. They also don't like apologizing and very often misinterpret things women say or do, so make sure you talk clearly to them and say things literally.

19. Try not to settle. You should know what you deserve and not settle for less. If you are dreaming for the man, who would love you the way you are, who would think you are most beautiful in the morning when you wake up; the one, who would respect you even if he doesn't agree with you on everything you say, the one, who would constantly inspire you and who is as ambitious as you are; the one, who will let you have your own life without trying to cage you; the one, who would trust you and

care. Once you meet that person, he will get under your skin for good. We all have certain type of energy and we always respond to the same kind of energy we exude ourselves. People sense our energy and decide whether they like it or not. They are either attracted to it or not. When you are happy, you attract happy people and the opposite.

20. Make sure you really want that guy before making any efforts to make him fall in love with you. Stay away from men who have cheated and abused women in the past. They will cheat on you and on everyone else. There are men, who like other men better than women, even though they would never admit it even to themselves. There are men, who are pathological liars and men who never do what they say they will and never call when they are supposed to. There are men, who are angry and bitter about everything all the time. There are men, who have been abused in the past and want to abuse someone in the present. Damaged people spend their lives being damaged. They would never change no matter what impression they create. They will not change for you or for anyone else. They wouldn't do all that bad stuff to you because it's you. They would do it to anyone. It's just who they are. It has nothing to do with you. Don't even try to date those men, as you

will only end up hurting yourself. Even though every man falls in love sooner or later, and he might fall in love with you, in a long run, you don't want to be with someone like that. Such men will make you feel lonely and desperate. Don't ever try to fix them. It's a waste of time. People can change their hair, looks, habits, manners and opinions, but they can't change who they are.

21.   Before you make someone fall in love with you, you should make yourself likeable and lovable. And that could only happen if you really like and love yourself. One has to like you first before they could feel something for you.

CHAPTER II
WHAT MEN LIKE AND DISLIKE. WHAT WORKS ON ALMOST ANY MAN OUT THERE AND MAKES HIM FALL IN LOVE.

IN THE BEGINNING:

There is no such thing as one strategy, which works on all men, because men are different, but some work on most men.

First date is certainly the most important date you would ever have with a man, and clearly, it has to go well, in order for a relationship to have a chance developing.

1.　Use reverse psychology – if you tell him: "Don't fall in love with me", he most likely will do just the opposite and he will not be able to help it. He will fall for you without even realizing it.

2.　The way you talk is important. You should talk in a way that everyone could understand what you are saying. Finish every sentence you start. Many American girls would fall in love with any other English guy for example, just because they love British accent. So no matter how charming you are, if someone doesn't like Jersey accent, Brooklyn accent, Long Island accent or foreign accent, they would hardly fall in love with you. And remember - it's more important how you say it than what you say.

3.　Your posture is very important. Stand straight. Walk as a Hollywood star, as a Super Model on the catwalk. You should look happy, confident and healthy.

4.　Men love narcissistic women, no matter they would deny it. So don't ever forget to love yourself more than you love him. Vanity in normal quantities is just fine. He will never love you if he senses you don't love yourself. In whatever way you treat yourself, the same way a man is going to treat you.

5.   Look at him in a way he can't resist. Usually a glance is what makes people fall in love. The glance releases a chemical (PEA), which is associated with falling in love. Look the man you like in the eyes and be present. Don't look through him and don't think of something else while you are with him, because he will immediately sense it and as a result, he will not like you back. Try making an eye contact, then look at his body, smile and look back in his eyes again. And hold a steady eye contact with him. Your eyes should never show fear or nervousness. Keep eye contact while talking to him.

6.   Men like shining eyes and large pupils because they make a woman look mysterious. Make your eyes shine for him.

7.   Hold his hand for a little longer than usual when shaking hands. That will make him feel you closer and he will think you are flirting with him.

8.   Touch him casually, whisper and wink at him. But don't be too touchy and don't hang on him too much in public. Most men don't like that, unless they are very affectionate themselves and are too much in love.

9. If you begin a movement towards him and stop it in the very last moment before you touch him, he will continue your movement and will touch you himself instead. This will create a romantic tension between both of you.

10. Wear red dress, high heels and long earrings. Red is the color of passion. It attracts men. Men find women, wearing red more attractive. However, red doesn't look good on everyone. But if it looks good on you, definitely wear it as much as you can. Scientists believe that men associate red with sexual arousal.

It matters how you look, smell and move – he will either be attracted or not.

11. Never use one of those super "clever" worn out pick-up lines, unless you want to sound extremely dumb. If you are determined to start the conversation first, just ask him a normal question or ask him to help you with something.

12. Smile and laugh a lot. Make yourself glow. Your body language should show him you desire him. You should be healthy first of all – healthy skin, healthy body and spirit. If you have any diseases, you can take care of them yourself. Read

"How to Get Rid of Any disease, Including Cancer Permanently" by Victoria Parker (Amazon.com).

13.   Men prefer to go on a date with a woman, who is interested in them and who is warm and sweet. Men think of such women as more feminine.

14.   Give. Withdraw. Then do it all over again. When you give – give from your heart – generously without expecting anything in return. Then withdraw to let him miss you, but make sure you have a reason to do so. Let two weeks pass by and then give again.

15.   Instead of boasting with your accomplishments, show him that you are pleasantly surprised by him – that is the best way to make a good first impression. He will feel intuitively that you would respond to his feelings and will be attracted to you.

16.   Create magnetism by using special words, which add flair like special, dreamy, passionate, exquisite, magical, magnificent, etc.

17.   Adapt yourself to what your man likes. Follow the rules he sets up for you. He will love you more if you enjoy what he enjoys. Focus on him and talk about his interests, not yours.

18.   Don't talk about anything negative. As much as people get attracted to watching and

reading bad news, no man would really like you if you talk about bad things all the time. Let him associate you with something positive instead.

19.   Do not try too hard to please him. That can't end up any good. He will lose interest in you immediately.

20.   Let him shine. He is the man. Make him feel that.

21.   Be feminine. Let him feel generous and strong while you are together. He would treat you always well if you let him lead. Absolutely don't try to get the check, especially on a first date. Just thank him. A man, who really likes a woman will never let her pay.

22.   Don't talk about children or about commitment at least in the beginning.

23.   There is that rule you've heard and read about - to not talk and ask about previous relationships too early on. Finding out what women he likes is a good thing, as you will save a lot of time, which you hardly have in excess, instead of having to wait for weeks to find out that the reason he split with his ex was that they were both completely different people and as a matter of fact, his ex was exactly like you and likes the same things you like and which he hates. Of course, if your ex

left you because of another woman, and there was too much craziness in your previous relationship, you'd probably rather keep that to yourself on a first date or else, you will be associated with "crazy" and he will not be calling you again.

24. Find out what he looks for in a woman, his favorite food, music, books and movies. Find out what he dreams for, what his fantasies are, what he respects in other men and women.

25. Don't look at your phone or text while you are with him. Focus on him only and that's the only way to connect with him. Give him your full attention. That will make him want to be with you.

26. Make a hint that you have many admirers and act like a prize.

27. Men like women, who have already been found to be desirable by others. It is very easy for a man to get convinced that he wants you if he knows you are sought-after. Only then he thinks you are really worth seeking.

28. Be easy to be with. Let him feel it is a pleasure being with you. Be lighthearted and not too serious.

29. Never criticize a man overtly. No one likes criticism, including the man you are on a date with. That would make him unsecure and resistant to any

kind of change. You should suggest changes and ideas instead.

30.   Compliment him. Male ego is very fragile and is usually equal to the ego of a teenager.

31.   Talk nice about people, even about the ones who talk bad about you. He will be impressed with your grace.

32.   Show him that you trust him. Trust him when he tells you he is true to you and he loves you. Otherwise, you will be showing him that you know you are replaceable. He will do his best to keep your trust for the future as well.

33.   Encourage him to pursue his goals. Don't try to manage him. Let him take his own decisions.

34.   Believe in a man and you will own his heart. Admire all his achievements, accept him the way he is and appreciate any single thing he does. Once you show him you believe in him, he will get wings. He will achieve anything.

35.   When we see someone often, it amplifies our likes or dislikes. Men are more likely to fall in love at first sight than women and the more they see that woman, the more they like her. Once there is a repeated exposure and a man sees you often, he likes you more. Similar to the fact that we like actors and politicians we see on TV. If he doesn't like you to

start with, though, repeated exposure would only have the opposite effect.

36. There should be some similarity at least between you both and you should help him see it. Similarity makes men more comfortable in the relationship. If you have a similar behavior, background and temperament, you will be more likely to get together and stay together.

37. Try to date a few men, even if it is against your principles at least in the beginning. Otherwise, you might get too attached and focused on one man only and he would sense it. Chances are your attention would scare him away and he would be soon gone. Don't make your plans around one man only. The only person you should really love and make plans around is you.

38. Be charismatic. Everyone gets excited by charismatic people. They are happy with their lives and they have that special sexual energy, which drives everyone crazy about them. They all have that air of mystery, which it so rare and which everyone gets attracted to.

39. Make him talk about himself and the longer he talks about himself, the more interesting he will think you are. Focus your attention on him, not on yourself. The more he talks and the more you listen

to him – the more he will like you, though a big part of it is a matter of personality, chemistry and personal preference. Some people like to be entertained instead – they like to be around women, who talk too much.

40.   Once you satisfy a man's curiosity and stop being mysterious, in most cases, he will lose interest in you. Don't share too much. Don't try to sell yourself. Make him think that only if you decide, you could tell him a lot. If you feel a desire to brag, stop it. Once you start trying to make a man like you, he will feel it immediately and you will lose your strength.

41.   Be energetic. Men get drawn to and gravitate towards women with a lot of energy. Some psychiatrists believe that men receive a lot of energy from women during sex, while women get drained at the same time. When a woman is with many men, she gives out her energy to each one and doesn't have much left to herself.

42.   Never compete with a man. Very few women know this. Majority of men fall in love with women, who help them appear at their best. The more silly you are on what he is good at – the more you will allow him to impress you and he will end up being impressed by you. Never point out man's

shortcomings. And never, I repeat absolutely never hold him up to ridicule, especially in front of other people, unless you want him to really hate you till the end of his life.

43.   Never ever show a man you are emotionally dependent on him. That will be a huge turn off to him.

44.   Men like mystery. They like most the women they don't understand. Don't say exactly what you want. Let him try to guess. Leave it to his fantasy and his fantasy will no doubt do the rest. Create mystery without being too direct about what you want and where you are headed to.

45.   Thank a man for any invitation, but don't accept it each time. Be happy to see him, but don't be free for him each time he wants to see you. Keep him in suspense, at least in the beginning of the relationship.

46.   Try to tell him the least about yourself, while finding out as much as you can about him. Most men adore mystery and love women, which they can't figure out. They associate the ones who are easy to be understood with boring. Men love elusive girls, the ones, who are difficult to keep around. Do some men love it when women open up to them and does that make them hooked? Of course, but that's

not for everyone. Only a mature man, who is already extremely interested in you, could handle listening to your touching memories.

47. Don't mention your problems, at least not in the beginning – men don't like listening about problems (they already have enough at their work place), unless they already care about you a lot or they are the type, who love fixing and helping other people. Any other man would be scared away.

48. Never complain. Be positive. Don't nag and don't get angry out of small things. No one likes ill temper.

49. Don't try to justify yourself. You did what you thought was right and no further justification of your behavior is necessary.

50. Accept a man for who he is. Close your eyes for his shortcomings. Once you accept him, he will be willing to change.

51. Surprise him in a pleasant way. This is the fastest way to make him fall in love with you, before he could even gather his thoughts on what he thinks about you. Reveal some secret to him or do something nice he would never expect.

52. If a man doesn't call, don't freak out on him. Just pretend you didn't notice, the way you wouldn't

notice whether someone you don't care about calls or doesn't.

53.   Should you see him every night? It depends. There are men, who get attached and they want to see you and no one else every night. They want to be with you every free second they have. They are smart. They are monogamous. If you have such man next to you, certainly, see him as often as you want, every night is a good option. If you are with a man, who gets bored easily, doesn't get attached and likes to chase, you should see him only once a week.

54.   Don't ask a lot from a man in the beginning, because the more you ask for, the less he would feel giving you. Let him give you what he wants.

55.   Don't make your intentions obvious. Show him you glow of happiness when you see him, but don't say it with words, don't talk about it. Let your eyes express it instead. Your body language should be the only language, showing that you like him.

56.   Dignity is one of the most attractive qualities in a woman, which attracts a man. Never forget that and never sacrifice your dignity for anything.

57.   All men want to be appreciated and understood. Make him feel that way.

58.   Respect him. You don't have to always agree with what he says, but you have to always listen to

him and hear his opinion. Never try to belittle him. Always discuss all matters in private and never in front of friends and family. Be diplomatic and tactful.

59. Look up to him. According to a research, most men have confessed they've cheated with someone, who was less attractive than their current partner. Why? Because the object of their affair looked up to them at their work place and made them feel flattered and wanted.

60. Keep your intelligence to yourself and don't boast with it, at least in the beginning. Don't try to show him how intelligent you are. Intelligence is not something that would make him fall in love with you, unless he is from the minority of men, who really appreciate that quality. Anything you are trying to sell about yourself makes you just more insecure. Don't try to prove anything to him. You can't hide intelligence and a smart man will notice it immediately anyway.

61. Don't be a "know-it-all". People, who think they know everything better than anyone else are unattractive to either sex. No one could be always right, including you.

62. Be confident. Everyone is drawn to confident people, no exceptions here. Be indifferent to what people think about you.

63. Don't appear to care too much about him and that approach can make miracles and take way further any regular woman, than if she was exceptional, but crazy about him. Be a challenge.

64. A man can only listen to a woman with attention for approximately 20 seconds. So start with the most important thing you want him to hear.

65. Be enthusiastic about anything, unless he offers you to take drugs or something as crazy.

66. Be busy. Have your own life. Meet with your friends and family; go to events. Have your own hobbies and passions. That way you will have your own excitement and he will respect you more. Men are attracted to women, who have their own life and who have a lot of positive things going on in that life.

67. Be tolerant. No one is perfect. Learn to compromise.

68. Don't ever invade his personal space. He will hate you for that.

69. Get him to do you a small favor. Men love to be able to help.

70. Men don't like needy women. Don't ask him to hold your hand all the time and tell you how

much he loves you. Don't require 24/7 emotional and moral support.

71.   No man likes a woman, who talks bad about other women. Women in general have a problem of saying how beautiful another woman is.

72.   If a man starts telling you about other women stalking him and sending him angry messages, beware. It's very likely he is exaggerating, or he actually deserves those angry messages, because he has acted like a jerk.

73.   Don't try to sell yourself, as then you make it obvious that you like him. Your getting under his skin should be insidious.

74.   Let him be himself. Let him spend time with his friends, go to sports events, etc. Try to like his friends and make sure they like you back. Don't expect him to give up his friends for you. What if a guy is in his 30's or 40's and still gathers religiously with his guy friends a few times a week, including Saturday nights? What if he goes to concerts with his guy friends instead of with you? Yes, there are men like that who enjoy hanging out with other guys more than they do with women. In the end, men always do whatever they decide. If this is a deal breaker for you – just leave him. Don't try to change

him. He will only hate you over it. If he can't make a space in his life for you, it means he doesn't want to.

75.   Don't apologize too much. Learn to like your flaws and do not apologize over them. Men usually take apologies the wrong way. They think if one apologizes, they are weak and they really did something wrong.

76.   Men like women, who don't come too close too soon.

77.   Don't friend request him on Facebook, unless you want him as a friend only.

78.   Be amiable, sophisticated and a bit spoiled. Be like Serene - dissociated from any kind of care.

79.   Have many friends in general, including girl-friends. Men like popular women, but beware – many men don't like party girls. So be careful what messages your behavior and actions convey to him.

80.   Treat him the same way you would treat a little boy. Nothing they share about themselves should intimidate you.

81.   Hint him you could give him what he wants. Not what you think he wants, but what he really wants. He will then get addicted to you. He will be happy to be with you all the time. He will be dreaming of you.

82. Don't be too nice or make him too many compliments, because when you do so, men think you want to sleep with them.

83. Play to his fantasies and show him you could satisfy his needs if you wanted to.

84. Make him feel like he wants to be a better man.

85. Independent and powerful women are not a cup of tea for every man. Most men like feminine women, whom they could protect. Responsibilities make male energy stronger and female energy weaker. Most men don't like strong women.

86. Go to an exciting event together. It has been proven that when people are excited about some experience, for example, when they are at a concert of their favorite music band, they tend to like the person they are with at the concert much more, as they usually believe their excitement comes from the person they are with instead of from the band. When one's feelings are intensified and moved to an extreme, people fall in love much easier. This is what the psychiatrists call "misattribution of emotions". Whether it is a concert, a movie, a loss of a loved one, a great joy or fear, each time people are emotionally sensitive – they are more likely to fall in

love with the person, who is next to them at that time.

87.   The more desperate you are trying to please someone, the worse attitude you will get back in response.

88.   Know what you want and never change your values over a guy in order to please him.

89.   Learn to listen more than you talk. Ask questions. Show him that you care and that he is important. And don't offer advice, unless you are asked for it. Make it all to be about him, not about you.

90.   Never ask him "What do you think". He will not tell you anyway, but the chances are he will get seriously annoyed.

91.   Some men, usually the ones with a high Emotional Intelligence and the ones who are compassionate get aroused by vulnerable women. Many men will love you for your weaknesses. However, there are emotionally damaged men, who will hate you when they see you weak and vulnerable and would use it against you as much as they can.

92.   Don't make jokes and don't be sarcastic with a man. As much as men like to make jokes about other people, they hate someone making jokes on

their own back. As odd as it sounds, men don't like funny women. It's good to have a sense of humor and laugh at his jokes, but that doesn't mean you have to try to be funny and tell jokes all the time. Women are attracted to funny men, because in order to be really funny, one has to be intelligent. Women appreciate intelligence in men, but men in general are not attracted to intelligence or at least they don't connect humor to intelligence.

MEN AND CHALLENGES:

93. Men love women, who make them stay on their toes. When a man knows a woman for a long time and gets to know her well, the charisma loses its impact. Men lose interest and feel disenchanted. Create a challenge to get back his interest or just move on.

94. Men believe they love danger and challenges, though that might not necessarily always be the case, but they like elusive women, because those women are the ones, who create that feeling of danger. Men like to chase and conquer and they get that pure basic excitement each time they head blindly towards danger. If you are not scared of danger yourself, you would be way more attractive to a man.

95. Most men always want what they can't have. They like to gamble and they love women, who can give them that sweet feeling of uncertainty. Men love knowing that they have to make efforts to keep you at any moment. That's when they feel alive. Men are drawn to women who they feel they can lose any moment.

96. You should always be aloof and never really let a man know that he is of too much importance to you.

97. Men like competition and adore risks and difficulties. They need to know that they have to fight for you and you are desired by many others.

98. Most men never think with their head and rarely choose the good girl, who would make them happy. They usually choose the one, who inflames them and who they know very well, will break their hearts. Most men have that delusional way of thinking that bad girls are exciting and sexy and they associate good girls with boring and predictable.

99. For some reason men believe that bad girls would be good in bed, which is certainly not true, but don't try to convince them they are wrong. They would never believe you.

100. Passion is ignited by insecurity. Most men like to feel unsecure and that makes their hearts racing. They feel alive. Once they start thinking they have you, they lose interest.

101. Never let a man think that there are no other men in your life. Men dream of women, who are popular and hard to get.

102. Turn him down from time to time. Tell him you would love to spend time with him, but you have plans already.

103. Many men can't imagine the relationship too far ahead. They like to be with someone, who would provide them with the maximum amount of fun with zero responsibilities and will not push them to commit to anything.

104. Men like emotional pain, though they would always deny it. But yes, they do enjoy taking the risk of being treated badly and getting hurt. For some reason, men believe that being with a bad girl will be an amazing experience, even though it's bad for them.

105. Men are competitive and not very rational when it comes to love. They associate "difficult to get" with "special" and "worth it", which is certainly not the case, but go explain it to them. When it costs them a lot to have you, they think you are more

beautiful. They want to conquer you. If you are easily had, his competitive ego will not be challenged, his adrenalin will not be raised.

SHOULD YOU PLAY HARD TO GET?

106. Should you be hard to get or not? Playing hard to get can work only if a man is already at least a little bit interested in you for one reason or another and not yet in love with you. When you are hard to get, that increases the desire of a man to catch you.

107. An aloof woman is wanted more, but at the same time, a man likes her less. Why? Because he sees she is unlike a normal human being, who would respond right back to his messages and who would like him back, so his ego is in a way hurt.

108. While trying to play games, you take the risk to look rude and un-respectful.

109. Once a man has already invested in a relationship, and you get hard to get at that point, he is way more likely to chase you, than if you are hard to get in the very beginning and he is not yet that interested to make any efforts at all to chase you. Once a man already likes you, playing hard to get would increase his interest in you. He would chase you once he knows he likes you and he has

already invested at least a little bit in you and when you are not overly available, he would perceive you as more interesting. It's a human thing to want more what one can't have. If you are hard to get initially, a man would most probably not like you. But if you are easy to get, pleasant and sweet in the beginning, he would think you are a wonderful human being who is worth investing feelings in.

110. Playing hard to get works, because men like the ones, who are more difficult to obtain. They like when they have to work for you. A woman, who was difficult to get would be valued way more that the one, who came up easily. But if you are hard to get before they even know they like you, they would hardly make any effort to chase you.

111. Be glamorous and elusive. Be energetic rather than bored and lethargic. Demonstrate your value.

112. Avoid sharing a lot of details of your life with him at least earlier on in the relationship. The less he knows – the better.

113. In order for him to fall in love with you, he has to not only like you a lot when you meet, but he also needs to have a bit of a doubt whether he could have you later on. For that purpose, you should elude him, make him think you are not interested in

him and not give him a definite answer. If he is sure he can have you any time, he will not be fully into you – as stupid as it sounds, that's how men react when it comes to romance.

114. His imagination is what helps him fall in love. And his imagination works best when you are not with him – that is when he can dream about you, associate you with something legendary and therefore overvalue you.

115. Awaken his instinct as a hunter. Conquering women, desired by other men is always sweeter to a man. When you don't give in easily, he would be stimulated to catch you.

ABOUT HAVING SEX WITH HIM:

116. Intimacy is not a formula for a successful relationship. Dignity is. You have to have self control and emotional stability at any time.

117. A man can really appreciate a woman only if he has to wait before he has sex with her. Delay the moment you will have sex with him. Make him wait, unless he is one of those guys, who get attached after they have sex (there are just very few of them).

118. The best time to have sex with him is after you both have decided you want to be in an exclusive committed relationship.

119.   Tell him that you are not interested in a relationship and he will try to change your mind.

120.   The first time you have sex, don't show him every single trick you know in bed, but rather be unskilled. Wear white underwear (not too sexy one).

ONCE YOU ARE IN A RELATIONSHIP:

121.   The more of his time and money a man spends on you, the more he will love you, no matter what he says. So make him invest in you. Men are very vain. They enjoy taking care of their women. Allow them to do so. They like it when you are financially dependent on them. Of course, you shouldn't cross the line and ask for too much too soon. If you don't allow a man to take care of you, you take away a big part of his interest in you. As much as independent spiritually you should be, allow yourself to be financially dependent on him. The more a man does for you, the more he becomes attached to you. Teach him to give you gifts. The more he gives you – the more he will love you. By giving you a gift, a man invests in you. Ask for gifts in person only. Compliment his faultless taste when you receive a gift from him.

122.   Be soft and feminine. When you are soft and sweet, he will not show you his aggressive side. He

will treat you like a woman and he will want to protect you, instead of treating you like a partner. He will not try to compete with you. When he feels powerful around you, he will want to fulfill all your wishes.

123. Never remind a man of his failures, as you will deprive him of all his energy.

124. Do not try to convince him in anything, because he will become resistant instead. Do not give him any advice on anything. Never self-sacrifice for a man or else he will feel you are like a mother to him. He will stop desiring you.

125. Men don't like overly jealous women. A little bit is Okay – you show that you care, but if it grows beyond control, it is appalling to him.

126. Show him that you are not afraid to be without him.

127. Don't be too emotional because to a man "emotional" means "crazy". Don't ask why. Their brains are just wired differently. Emotions scare men. They don't know how to deal with them.

128. Use all of your energy to yourself. Don't teach him and don't give him advice on everything.

129. Be in control of yourself, your behavior and emotions in any possible situation.

130. Never take offence if you want to win. Taking offence makes you lose your authority. Don't waste your energy on offences. Don't let insults get to you.

131. If your man had an affair and you decide to stay with him after, don't punish him forever. Don't allow guilt and anger stay between both of you.

132. If he tells you he needs space, give it to him. It doesn't necessarily mean that he wants to break up with you. He might just want to get in touch with himself.

133. Create distance and he will start getting nervous about losing you. Give him space. More than he would ever need. That would keep him closer to you than if you tried to make him stay close.

134. Be always happy. He should feel he is free to go at any time.

135. Don't ever try to change him. At least don't make it obvious.

136. Learn to like his friends and family. That is very important to him.

137. Make sure you don't ignore reality and put him on a pedestal in your mind. He could hardly live up to your expectations.

138. Never tell a man he made you cry or you are unhappy or miserable because of him. A man would

start hating you if you do so – he would think you are possessive.

139.   Never ask a man how he feels about you.

140.   Make a man always feel like he wants to impress you. Once he stops feeling that way, it will be the end.

141.   Be sensual. Men like sensual women.

142.   Never embarrass a man. You may get him angry at you from time to time, which is a good thing, but never ever embarrass him.

143.   Don't post to social media too much. That only makes people think you don't have a life. Be at least a little bit mysterious.

144.   Find a way to make him miss you. He will over-valuate you if he thinks he lost you or he wonders whether you still like him.

145.   Absence is very good for a man to start missing you. But the absence should come rather later in a relationship than earlier on.

146.   Men usually desire more everything forbidden. If he thinks you are forbidden, he would want you more.

147.   Never show ill temper. Be elegant even when you are angry. Never use words and comments you will later regret. Never show your anger in front of other people. Whatever went wrong should be

discussed between both of you only. Don't mention past events you've already discussed and don't use belittling comments.

148. If he believes he could play with your feelings and be rewarded after, he would never fall in love with you.

149. Don't be in a hurry to discard all of your admirers because of him, because otherwise he will discard you first. You will not be glamorous to him any more if you don't seem desired by others. Men are too superficial to appreciate you if they think they are the only ones, who want you.

150. Talk his language. Use the same words and terminology he does. That makes him feel like you come from the same background. Have the same reaction as him – laugh at what he laughs, agree with his comments on things, so he understands you share similar values. Laugh at his jokes and be interested in whatever he is interested.

151. Stand closer to him than you stand to other people, the way friends do.

152. When you have your life and not let him in it all the time, he believes you are more attractive.

153. Make him feel good about himself. He will love you more.

154. The easiest way to get the love spell broken is to become too nice and predictable. Unless you alternate the pleasure you give and your kindness with inflicting some pain, it will not have a happy end. From a man's perspective, the moment you become too predictable, you become boring and undesired. The only way to go from here is to change your behavior and take the relationship to a different direction.

155. Never say "you don't call me enough" or "tell me you love me". Be unpredictable. A man should never be able to figure you out. Men like women they can't understand and they can't control. Never make him tell you he loves you. If he feels that way, he will tell you that himself.

156. Never give yourself fully. Always make a man keep guessing.

157. Men usually fall in love with women they rescue. Allow your man to rescue you from something.

158. Show a man attention, let him make decisions, admire him and act as if he is the very best, trust him and rely on him, be capricious, don't show up for appointments sometimes.

159. Your man wants recognition. Give it to him. Encourage his best self. Inspire him to grow, to

work, to open new companies, to make money, to become a better person.

160. Men need time to fall in love, so if it doesn't happen immediately, don't panic. It will come with the time.

161. A man can't do shopping for more than 30 minutes, so if you are planning to take him shopping, make sure he doesn't lose patience before you even get there.

162. Usually, when one of the partners strikes/freaks out on the other one, it is because they are starved for love.

163. If he does something wrong, tell him it makes you angry and ask him what solution he offers to fix things instead of yelling at him. That way you don't blame him directly and you turn the problem to him. He sees that it's up to him to change things for the better.

164. You will attract a man with a promise of passion, but you have to become elusive and un-accessible right after.

165. Don't get a man get too comfortable and lazy. Show him he can't keep you unless he makes efforts to do so. When a man is attracted to you, he feels motivated to keep you and please you.

166. Many women start drama because they want attention and they think it will make things interesting, but what actually happens is, they start looking crazy instead and lose the guy's interest. He ends up thinking they are emotionally unstable.

167. The only place where you could allow him to be in full control of you is in the bedroom. Never let him make decisions for you bigger than what to order for you at the restaurant, where to take you on holidays or which movie to see. All major decisions in your life should be taken by you or mutually, not by him only.

168. When it comes to relationships, the one who cares less holds all the power.

169. Don't obsess over him no matter what. Never act needy and never be too accommodating and helpful.

170. Be independent emotionally and spiritually. Don't hang on him all the time. Show him you are able to function without him. Learn to be comfortable in your own skin. Don't be constantly after him, as he will feel suffocated and will leave you. Be able to enjoy life without him. You may miss him, but don't depend on him emotionally.

171. Don't give out your personal space for him. Never change your morals and values because of

him or else he will not respect you. There are always exceptions, of course. If he is Jewish and he asks you to convert, because his religion and his family request so, you might want to consider doing it if he is Mr. Right. Ivanka Trump did it for her husband. You should be able to do so too.

172. Don't look for someone to complete you. You should be a complete person yourself and it's great to meet someone, who would be your perfect companion, but you don't need someone who is not complete themselves as well. A relationship is not a place where people should try to find themselves.

173. Never sacrifice your dreams over a man, unless the man is exceptional and un-replaceable. Otherwise, you will regret it deeply one day.

174. When you have certain matters to discuss, only do it at 4 eyes. Never through text messages. People most often miscommunicate when writing and reading.

175. It is great to be in love and follow your heart, but don't forget to use your brain for the whole time. No matter how much you are in love, if your brain tells you that this person is not good for you, that he is only using you, or you are both completely incompatible and want different things from life, don't marry him, don't buy an apartment together

with him. You'd rather have your heart broken today than 10 years from now, when your chances to meet a quality man would not be the same.

176. Allow everything to happen naturally. Don't create timelines: don't tell him that since you've already dated a certain amount of time, it's time to get married. If he feels he wants to marry you, he will ask you on the second day after you've met. If he doesn't ask you within the timeline you've created yourself, just leave him and move on. There are no guidelines, no rules and no timelines when it comes to relationships. It takes 2 people to be ready to move forward.

177. Close your eyes for his mistakes and flaws as much as you can. Look beyond the small things and work towards creating a future together instead.

178. You have heard you shouldn't judge a man based on his past, but just help him live with it and move on instead. That sounds very lovely and spiritual. And if you really think that a person would create a different future with you, go ahead and do so. However, in order for you to protect yourself, don't show him that you take in consideration his past, but if you chose to completely ignore it, you are taking the risk of getting yourself deeply hurt. If he tells you how he cheated on his ex or someone

else in the past, you might think that he would never do that to you, but he will. If he told you how he tried to destroy his ex when she broke up with him, he will try to destroy you under the same circumstances as well. Don't fool yourself. People don't change.

179. The more alcohol he has had, the more attractive he will find you. Scientists have proven that alcohol changes the perception of attractiveness in people.

180. Love and acceptance are different things. One may love someone, but it doesn't mean they accept them and they would marry them.

181. Never push a man to do something he doesn't want to do.

182. When you fight, don't take sex away from him for a long time, as he will look for it and find it somewhere else.

183. You don't have to agree with everything he says, because men usually get bored at that point.

184. Always remain calm and objective.

185. At any moment he must know that you don't need him, but it is your choice to be with him rather than all other admirers you have.

186. Men like independent women. Don't change your taste for him. In other words, don't lose your identity for him.

187. Majority of men would take a woman for granted once they have no doubts she belongs to them.

188. Use phrases like: "You make me feel safe", "I am proud of you", "You make me happy", "You look amazing" to make him obsessed with you.

189. Most men like expensive women. Once you stop being expensive and turn to common, he will most likely lose interest in you. You will not be worth the effort to him any longer.

IF HE ACTS LIKE A JERK:

190. If he tries to bs you, remind him that no one is forcing him to stay with you. He is free to go at any time. He will respect you way more than anyone else if you don't tolerate his lies.

191. Show him that he can't mistreat you. Otherwise he would never respect you or fall in love with you.

192. If he acts as a jerk, no contact is the most powerful thing you could do – way more powerful than any word you would say. No contact is what

drives men crazy. Bad text messages have the opposite effect of what's intended.

193. Never reward a man for behaving badly towards you. If he acts like a jerk, don't try to show him more love, affection and attention. Don't show him how much you miss him. Don't tell him you love him, or else he will always treat you badly from then on. Only show him love when he acts appropriately and deserves it.

194. Don't show a man any negative attention – negative attention is way more rewarding than no attention at all.

195. Leave him. Break up with him and make him miss you. If he cannot live without you, he will come back to you begging you. And if you are gone, stay gone. Don't call him. Stand your ground. And he will come back, even if it had to take years for that to happen. If he is right for you, he will come back soon. He will realize he has been a jerk. Show him that you respect yourself.

196. Never ever send him a closure plea – this is the biggest mistake all women make. Men perceive closure pleas needy and desperate to a fault. Closure pleas never have the effect women expect – they always create exactly the opposite effect on men. Don't beg him to come back and don't apologize.

IF IT'S OVER BUT YOU STILL LOVE HIM AND WANT HIM BACK:

When people break up with someone, they rarely give out the actual reason. If he breaks up with you, it will probably be over something else, different from whatever reasoning he gave you.

197. Men usually mean what they say and if he says he doesn't want to see you anymore, believe that. Sometimes they would only want to break up with you for the only reason you are too nice and too available.

198. Don't call him, don't text him, don't initiate making plans with him. Don't make any movements towards him. Go silent. That would keep him guessing what you are thinking and will make him feel insecure. Don't let him lose respect for you by keeping on calling him and texting him.

199. If a man hurts you in some way, don't be in a hurry to respond. Give yourself space instead and show him that yow will not lash back at him. He will either understand he has acted as a jerk and will apologize, or he will not and if he doesn't, you don't need him anyway.

200. Don't show up at places where you know he will be. Do the opposite - avoid him.

201. Don't like his photos on Facebook or Instagram. Men perceive that as desperate.

202. Understand why he broke up with you. What did you do wrong? Unless you know what went wrong and how to change it, there is no point of trying to get back with him – it will end again.

203. Wait at least 30 days before you reach out to him. In the meantime concentrate on yourself. Life goes on. Try to date other people, meet with friends, go to the gym and make sure you don't isolate yourself.

204. Forgive him. If you are bitter, even if you get back together, it will never work out. Let go of all the anger inside of you. Accept him for who he is.

205. If you initiate contact in 30 days and he agrees to see you, make sure you look great, but don't overdo it, because he will think you are trying too hard and that will make him lose interest again.

206. Don't sleep with him too quickly after you decide to go back together. Wait for a while if you want to have a stronger connection this time.

MEN ARE DIFFERENT AND THEY GET ATTRACTED TO DIFFERENT THINGS

I am against generalizing people, and yet, even though there are many exceptions with all generalizations, some men are emotionally smart and some - stupid; there are intelligent men and there are men, who hate to think and read; there are successful men and there are the ones, whom we all refer to as to losers. There are also many damaged men. There are men, who are completely empty on the inside – all they care about is what kind of clothes and bags a woman wears.

When you meet a man, find out whether he has any serious issues. If he is an alcoholic or abusive – make sure you lose him as soon as you can. Those things never change.

Some men like women with problems and like to feel saviors. Some like to chase. Others like drama. Some are generous and others are cheap – cheap not only with money, but cheap to tell you a good word either. Give your man whatever he wants – if he wants to chase you, give him that excitement. I know men, who would chase women till the moment a woman gives up and agrees to go out with them, at which point they lose interest and cancel the date.

There is also category of men, who like to help and fix women the same way there are women, who like to fix men.

There are also serial daters out there. Stay away from them. They are very charming, because they have been training for dating all of their lives. However, they are able to forget a woman the moment she leaves their place. Those men long for a constant change of their lovers. They need a new thrill every week. They are scared to be single, because they lack self esteem and are insecure when by themselves. Serial daters constantly need someone to validate their worth. You need a monogamous man, who would stay with you forever without checking out every girl out there and looking for a bigger better deal.

Confident men are less defensive and are able to be in monogamous relationships. They don't need to prove themselves all the time. Insecure people tend to play games and are players. They believe that once you really get to know them, you will be disappointed.

CHAPTER III

HOW TO MAKE AN EMOTIONALLY IMMATURE MAN FALL IN LOVE WITH YOU

Many men out there have the "Peter Pan Syndrome", or they never grow up emotionally. Those men could be in their 40's or 50's and they are still incredibly immature. Some of them appear to have everything – good looks, good job or business and a lot of money, but their brains are stuck somewhere in fifth grade or in high school in the best case scenario. They have had traumatic experiences in their childhood which has made them miss out on growing up, or sometimes they are just surrounded by the wrong friends, who wouldn't let them grow up. You can almost never change a man with a "Peter Pan Syndrome". The best thing you could do is walk away when you meet him no matter how attractive he seems to be. It could hardly end well. Those men are not able to see beyond their immaturity. They usually like to go out with 20 year old models, not necessarily because they care too much about those girls, but because they believe it is somehow good for their reputation to be seen with a pretty tall girl. I am sure you know 40-something year old men who often date 20-year old girls, who hardly speak the same language (both literally and metaphorically).

Those men fool themselves they could have any woman they want. They like to manage other people's money, own restaurants and night clubs, produce movies, climb mountains, fly private jets and party a few times a week. Some of those men even go that far to pay 20 year old models just to show up with them in public or fly groups of those girls on private jets to St. Barths, Punta, Ibiza, St. Tropez, etc., just so they could be seen with those girls, as they believe that would make everyone jealous. They don't realize how pathetic they actually appear in the eyes of other women.

Do these young chosen girls love these guys back? They love the money and the private jet part of them, but if you take that away from the man, there would be no love left.

Men who are available on the dating scene often belong to this group and for them in order to figure out they like you, they need to be manipulated, they actually beg to be manipulated. If you would be happy to live with one of those charmers, who can only appreciate you if you look like a teenager and are at least 5.9 feet tall, below are the rules, which can get you any emotionally immature man you want.

207. Most men like what they can't have, but that's especially true about the immature ones – they absolutely love to chase. It is hard to imagine why a man would feel compelled to chase a woman, who doesn't like him back and how is it possible at all to want someone, who doesn't want you back. As hard it is to understand, there are men are as silly as that. So give them the pleasure of chasing you.

208. Men with Peter Pan syndrome fall for women, who are bohemian, who are very young and the less they communicate – the better.

209. Some of these men often don't like and don't love themselves, so they don't believe anyone else can do so if they get to know them. Many of these men even hate themselves and don't believe they are worthy of love. So if they meet someone, who shows them they like them, they get confused and anxious. They think that the person will soon find out who they really are and will get disappointed.

210. The less self respect a man has, the less he likes a woman who is nice to him. So don't be nice to these men. They don't think they deserve someone

to be nice to them. The ones, who don't love themselves at all, fall for women, who treat them badly.

211. Have in mind that those men usually enjoy the chase, not you. Soon after they catch you, they will get bored and will look for another object to chase. You should decide whether you want to be with such man or not and if you are really into him, you should make sure to never let him know you love him.

212. These men love women, who play games. These men play games themselves, because they are scared that they are not worth other people's time and if other people find out that they are too available, too nice or too boring, they would never like them back.

213. Ask yourself: do I really want someone, who would love me, because he can't have me and has to chase me? Don't I want someone, who is able to appreciate me even after he has me and I am available at all times for him? Don't you want to be with the one, you want to spend your life with? The one, who will be there for you even when he has you every night next to him.

214. If the man you like is a fool and you want to be with one – the above techniques will do miracles. He will be yours – at least while you follow them.

CHAPTER IV

HOW TO MAKE A QUALITY MAN WITH HIGH SELF ESTEEM FALL IN LOVE WITH YOU

There are men, who actually like women, who like them back. They are smart about relationships, have high self esteem and only like women, who like them back. If you meet such man, you would be lucky with him. Those men know their self-worth and appreciate a woman who is nice to them. These men can recognize a quality woman the moment they see her and they could fall in love right away. These men love women, who love them back and get turned off by having to chase someone. Unfortunately, such men are harder to find as they are usually already happily married or in monogamous long-term relationships.

They know they are worth much and they appreciate a person, who is able to see their worth at first sight. Such men like people, who show them how they feel, instead of playing games and pretending to be cold, or just being cold.

215. If you want to be with an amazing quality man, you have to be a quality person yourself.

216. Be intelligent. An intelligent woman is desired by a quality man. She knows how to constantly surprise him in a good way.

217. Show him you are able to compromise. Don't expect a fairy tale. No one is perfect and no relationship is perfect.

218. Be faithful to him. Never be the first one to cheat.

219. Never indicate you want to end the relationship if that's not really what you want.

220. You have to give and receive in a relationship with a quality man. Don't be just a taker, as if so, it will end up soon.

221. If a man is smart and you are his type – you don't really need to do much, just be yourself and that'll do.

CHAPTER V

THINK ONCE AGAIN IF YOU REALLY NEED TO BE IN A RELATIONSHIP. IF YOU HAVE TO COMPROMISE TOO MUCH IN ORDER TO DO SO, THAT MIGHT NOT BE THE BEST OPTION FOR YOU.

222. Given that as of today, there are 37 million married cheaters as members on the Ashley Madison matchmaking website, you are probably not missing much if you are single.

223. Don't be afraid to be single and self-sufficient. A confident woman is never going into a relationship just because she feels alone or because of the sake of the relationship or because she needs validation.

224. A relationship is about growing and moving forward in life happier and more fulfilled than if being by yourself. If you are in a relationship, that is doing nothing for you or even worse - makes you feel bad about yourself, you should just move on. You don't need unnecessary drama and you don't need people, who can add no value to your life. You need to be surrounded by people who inspire you and make you feel good about yourself.

225. A good relationship brings out the best of you and makes you more motivated.

226. Never forget that the most beautiful, smart and confident women often don't have boyfriends, because they don't want to settle and because it is extremely difficult for them to meet someone who is worth their time.

The above being said, if you are an amazing human being, if you are beautiful on the inside, if you work on improving yourself all the time, if you are an interesting person, if you are confident and don't want a relationship at any rate and if you are willing to give him enough space - when you meet the right man, he will love you just the way you are!

Dear Reader, if you liked this book and it helped you in one way or another, I would really appreciate if you write a couple of words as a review.

Thank you!

Other Books from this Publishing House:

How To Get Anything You Want
The Ultimate Secrets on How To Get Money, Love, Luck and Health

Getting the Mystery of Success Solved

Victoria Parker

How to Get Rid of Any Disease, Including Cancer Permanently

More than 50 Scientifically Proven Therapies that cost almost nothing and Will Make You Healthy with No Side Effects

Victoria Parker

Printed in Great Britain
by Amazon